Compassioning

Basic Counselling Skills for Christian Care-Givers

Margaret Ferris, C.S.J.

Sheed & Ward

Sheed & Ward™ is a service of The National Catholic Reporter Publishing Company.

Library of Congress Cataloguing-in-Publication Data

Ferris, Margaret
    Compassioning : basic counselling skills for Christian care-givers / Margaret Ferris.
        p.   cm.
    Includes bibliographical references.
    ISBN 1-55612-567-4 (alk. paper)
    1. Pastoral counseling. 2. Spiritual direction. 3. Carkhuff, Robert R. 4. Caring--Religious aspects--Christianity. I. Title.
BV4012.2.F47 1993
253.5--dc20   92-39456
                                                               CIP

Published by: Sheed & Ward
              115 E. Armour Blvd.
              P.O. Box 419492
              Kansas City, MO 64141-6492

To order, call: (800) 333-7373

Contents

Preface v

Introduction vii

Chapter 1: Background and Overview of the Model 1

Chapter 2: The Pre-Helping Stage 5
      1. Physical Attending 5
      2. Psychological Attending 9
      3. Spiritual Attending 14
      Exercises in Attending Skills 15

Chapter 3: Stage I—Self-Exploration 18
      1. Respect 19
      2. Empathy 21
      3. Warmth/Caring 25
      Exercises in Stage I Skills 27

Chapter 4: Stage II—Self-Understanding 35
      1. Concreteness/Specificity 35
      2. Genuineness 37
      3. Self-disclosure 37
      4. Prayer 38
      The Global Scale of Responding 40
      Exercises in Stage II Skills 42

Chapter 5: Stage III—Action 45
      1. Confrontation 45
      2. Immediacy 48
      3. Support 49
      Exercises in Stage III Skills 52

Chapter 6: Referral Counselling 55
      1. Whom Should One Refer? 55
      2. Where and How to Refer 57

Conclusion 61

Appendix A: Some Useful Techniques for Helping 62
      1. Obtaining a Data Base 62
      2. Writing Therapy 63
      3. Imaginative Dialoguing 64

    4. Identifying Patterns and Themes   65
    5. Decision-Making/Discernment 66

Appendix B: Answers to Rating Exercises 70

Bibliography   72

Preface

A word which often comes to mind when one thinks of the pastoral ministry of Jesus is the word "compassion." It is a word which is rich in meaning yet one which defies adequate description. In fact, it is the word which Jesus used as an encompassing description of the Christian stance. Jesus' oft-quoted injunction to be perfect as God is perfect is more accurately translated in Luke as "be compassionate as God is compassionate" (Luke 6:36). If we study the word "compassion," we find that it comes from the Latin words *cum patior* which mean, among other things, to stand *with*, to undergo *with*, to share deeply *with* another or others. The emphasis here is on the preposition *"with."* Compassion is not pity which sometimes connotes condescension. No, there is a mutuality about compassion which carries with it a recognition of the other as holy. Moreover, compassion does not end at the feeling level but moves outward toward the alleviation of a suffering or the celebration of a joy.

This is the task of the Christian and more specifically of the Christian care-giver who openly espouses the task of "compassioning" others in their journey. Yet we sometimes find ourselves at a loss as how best to do this. I hope that the model presented in these pages will be helpful in this regard. It is one which is rooted in compassion in that it teaches us how to stand with others in their joys and sorrows and, through the resourceful use of *pastoral* counselling skills, gradually enable them to move outward,

v

fashioning for themselves appropriate healing attitudes and actions.

It is with great gratitude that I recall those who have "compassioned" me in my journey thus far—those numerous women and men who have taught me so much about the interrelationships of spirit, mind and body and enabled me to translate often ambiguous feelings into life-giving actions.

In particular, I wish to thank my students and all those who through the years have entrusted me with their stories. It is through them that I have come to know more fully the compassionate God who accompanies us.

To my teachers and classmates at the Graduate Theological Foundation in Donaldson, Indiana, I owe the motivation for this particular work. I am especially indebted to Martha Bartholomew, William Creed and John Simmons for their reading of and valuable feedback on the original manuscript. I also want to thank Dr. George Gazda and his associates at the University of Georgia for providing me with and allowing me to use several of the scales which they have developed in their work with teachers.

Finally, I wish to thank my family and my religious community, the Sisters of St. Joseph of London, whose consistent love and support have challenged me to take up this work of "compassioning" and who continue to model for me on a daily basis the very helping skills of which I speak in this model.

Margaret Ferris, C.S.J.

Introduction

Essential to both pastoral counselling and spiritual direction is the ability to master the art of facilitative listening. Like most beginners, when I first became involved in the work of spiritual direction, I put great energy into trying to discern how God was acting in the lives of those whom I was guiding. I also put great energy into worrying about whether I was doing things right or not. Unconsciously (perhaps even consciously!), I had in mind an image of the spiritual director as some sort of an all-knowing guru with a direct line to the Almighty. I knew that my connections were much less impressive than that, and the fact that people kept coming to me at that time for spiritual guidance is ample proof that the real director or guide in such a relationship is indeed the Holy Spirit.

Subsequently I enrolled in a graduate program in counselling and carried with me those same stereotypes of the all-knowing counsellor who was supposed to have the answers to everyone's problems. Fortunately, the model of counselling which was presented (the "Carkhuff Model") was one in which the counsellor simply facilitated the counsellee in reaching his or her own solution to the problem at hand, believing that in most cases, they had that power within themselves.

Another thing which amazed me at that time was the number of communication skills identified by the counselling model which we were using and the fact that they could actually be taught and learned in a systematic way. Counsellors were not "just born."

Even those who had a natural bent for the profession could learn much from this particular model.

In the years that followed, I began teaching this same model to beginning counsellors. I also continued doing spiritual direction and to my delight became aware of how much more helpful one could be when using this model. Later, as I moved into the teaching of pastoral counselling, I was forced to consider more intentionally how the spiritual and pastoral fit into all of this. From my research and reflections emerged the adaptation of the original model presented herein.

What I am attempting to do in this work is to present a simplified version of the original model and suggest points at which the spiritual can be introduced into it. I shall also present, where appropriate, some exercises for the development of the skills discussed. It is hoped that this work might be used with beginning pastoral counsellors and spiritual directors, as well as with other Christian care-givers, as a basic training model in communication skills—a model which integrates the spiritual into the psychological.

I have found the model to be particularly useful for those whom I refer to as "occasional pastoral counsellors," that is, those such as parish clergy and pastoral associates for whom pastoral counselling is not their sole profession but only one of the many responsibilities which fall to their lot.

I have also found the model helpful in the training of spiritual directors. Too often in such training, the emphasis is placed almost exclusively on such things as patterns of spiritual development, discernment of spirits, etc., to the neglect of basic communication skills.

The preferable way to use this model is as a teaching guide, progressing from chapter to chapter and skill to skill in regular weekly sessions with a group of trainees. The time between sessions can be used by trainees to practice the skills discussed and possibly to tape some practice interviews for critiquing by the trainer or by the training group. The model lends itself well to such things as a semester of seminary teaching or a unit of a spiritual direction training program. If one wishes to go more deeply into the model, I would recommend that the work of counselling psychologist George Gazda and his associates (to which I will allude in the next chapter) be used in conjunction with this work.

Having taught and used this model extensively over a period of more than twelve years, I can attest to its effectiveness in training both pastoral counsellors and spiritual directors. These are the two groups to whom I shall explicitly address myself in the body of this work. However, many of my colleagues have assured me that there are other Christian care-givers who could profit from this model—lay deacons, chaplains, various parish personnel—any persons, in fact, who are frequently called upon to lend a listening ear within a Christian context. I am sure that this is true and hope that this work will be instrumental in making all of us more compassionate and effective care-givers.

NOTE: In an effort to use inclusive language in the text, I have chosen in places to alternate the use of "he" and "she" where the use of "he or she," "himself or herself," etc., would prove cumbersome.

Chapter One

Background and Overview of the Model

1. Background

The effectiveness of the core model used in this manual has been well-demonstrated by extensive research. It owes its initial impetus to the work of Robert Carkhuff and C.B. Truax who investigated many different types of therapies and counselling models in order to determine if there were any particular counselling skills that were common to them all. Later, they joined up with Dr. Carl Rogers and a number of other researchers at the University of Wisconsin to produce the basis of the following model.[1]

This model, which generally became known as the "Carkhuff Model," was adapted by others such as Gerard Egan[2] and George Gazda and associates[3] to fit a wide range of helping situations. For purposes of the present work, I shall be drawing primarily on the form of the model presented by George Gazda and associates in their book *Human Relations Development: A Manual for Educators.* I have chosen this particular interpretation of the model because it is rightly alluded to as a *helping* model, rather than exclusively as a counselling model. As such, it lends itself not only to pastoral counselling but also to the art of spiritual direction and to other helping relationships.

1

In presenting this model, I am aware that the person using it for spiritual direction and/or pastoral counselling must be schooled in other aspects of those fields, such as spirituality, theology, scripture, developmental psychology, etc. My purpose here is simply to show how one can use the well-proven findings of psychology to enhance communication in the pastoral area and to show how these "helping skills" are essentially similar to those used by Jesus as he related in a compassionate, healing way with others.

2. Overview

The "Carkhuff Model" is a developmental model in which communication skills are used in a progressive manner which best facilitates openness and growth on the part of the helpee. (I am purposely using the terms helper/helpee in this work, rather than counsellor/counsellee or director/directee, to indicate that the model can be used in many different helping situations in the pastoral sphere.)

In the model as set forth by Carkhuff[4] and adapted by George Gazda and associates, there are three major stages or phases preceded by a pre-helping stage. A diagramatic representation of what I will henceforth refer to as the "Carkhuff-Gazda" model along with a diagrammatic representation of the adaptation of the model which I am proposing, is found on page 3 (Table I).

In the following pages, I will attempt to describe in more detail and in my own words the skills outlined in this model, to show how the spiritual or pastoral dimension fits into each stage and to suggest some exercises for training people in using this model. (In the text, discussion of the spiritual components which I have added appears in **boldface print**.)

As we examine the skills required of the helper at each stage of the model, it must be remembered that the skills are cumulative, that is, one does not use the skills of one stage up to a certain point in the interview and then leave them behind as one moves into the next stage. Rather, one continues to use the skills of the preceding stage(s), adding those of the next stage at the appropriate time. When one becomes proficient in the use of the model, one can draw on any of the skills at will. In fact, eventually the helper is no longer conscious of using the skills in a sequential order; they simply become a part of his or her manner of relating.

Table I: Summary of the "Carkhuff-Gazda" Model

Stage/Purpose	Helper Skills Necessary[5]
Pre-Helping Stage: -to create an atmosphere of openness conducive to sharing.	1. Physical Attending 2. Psychological Attending
Stage I: -to facilitate **self-exploration**	1. Empathy 2. Respect 3. Warmth/Caring
Stage II: -to deepen **self-understanding**	1. Concreteness/Specificity 2. Genuineness 3. Self-disclosure
Stage III: -to facilitate **action**	1. Confrontation 2. Immediacy

Summary of Model Adding Spiritual Dimension

Stage/Purpose	Helper Skills Necessary
Pre-Helping Stage: -same as above.	1. Physical Attending 2. Psychological Attending **3. Spiritual Attending**
Stage I: -same as above.	1. Respect (**Based on God-likeness**) 2. Empathy (**Rooted in compassion**) 3. Caring (**Flowing from love**)
Stage II: -same as above.	1. Concreteness/Specificity 2. Genuineness 3. Self-disclosure **4. Prayer**
Stage III: -same as above.	1. Confrontation (**Truth in love**) 2. Immediacy 3. Support (**Involving the Christian Community**)[6]

Notes

1. For further background on the origin and evolution of this model, see George Gazda et al, *Human Relations Development: A Manual for Educators*, Third Edition (Toronto: Allyn and Bacon, Inc., 1984), pp. 4-6.

2. Egan, Gerard, *The Skilled Helper: A Model for Systematic Helping and Interpersonal Relating* (Monterey: Brooks/Cole Publishing Company, 1975).

3. Gazda, George M. et al, *Human Relations Development: A Manual for Educators*, Third Edition (Toronto: Allyn and Bacon, Inc., 1984)

4. Carkhuff, R.R. 1971a. "Helping and Human Relations: A brief guide for training lay helpers." *Journal of Research & Development in Education*. 4(2), 17-27.

5. From George M. Gazda, Frank R. Asbury, Fred J. Balzer, William C. Chiders, and Richard P. Walters. *Human Relations Development: A Manual for Educators*. Fourth Edition. Copyright 1991 by Allyn and Bacon. Reprinted with permission.

6. "Support" is a skill which has been added to the "Carkhuff Model" by Gerard Egan (op. cit.). I have used it in my interpretation of the model because I find it a particularly important skill in both pastoral counselling and spiritual direction.

Chapter Two

The Pre-Helping Stage

Initial impressions are important in any helping relationship. This is particularly so in those relationships where people are feeling their vulnerability or wish to discuss sensitive matters—hence the importance of the pre-helping stage. In this phase of the helping relationship, one sets the stage, so to speak, for the whole interview. Before the helper opens his or her mouth, messages are conveyed, and a climate of facilitation is either created or impeded.

The helper skills identified by Carkhuff at this stage are Physical Attending and Psychological Attending. To these I have added Spiritual Attending, so that in this model the Pre-Helping Skills are:

1. Physical Attending
2. Psychological Attending
3. **Spiritual Attending**

1. Physical Attending

This refers to the way that we are bodily present to the helpee and to the physical arrangements of the meeting place—the environment. It includes such things as:

- the arrangement of furniture
- any physical barriers set up between the helper and the helpee

- non-verbal messages conveyed by the eyes, tone of voice, posture, mannerisms, gestures, energy-level, etc.

Let us take a more detailed look at some of the elements of physical attending which I have found to be particularly important, first discussing their general meaning in the context of the helping interview, then highlighting any points that might have special implications for pastoral counselling and/or spiritual direction.

Furniture

The setting in which the interview takes place should be simple but inviting. If it is one's office, the desk should be arranged in such a way as not to act as a barrier between helper and helpee. A "talking corner" or space should be set up with chairs which are comfortable enough to keep both helper and helpee alert. Some prefer swivel chairs which will enable both the helper and the helpee to change positions from time to time.

The meeting place should be relatively uncluttered. Too much clutter sometimes leads to cluttered thinking, something which one does not need in such a situation. On the other hand, the room should not be sterile but inviting. One's choice of pictures, books and other articles will give the helpee an impression about the helper before the interview even begins.

> **In pastoral counselling and spiritual direction, it is good to have some things in evidence which indicate that the spiritual side of the person is valued and will be respected—an open Bible, a crucifix, some spiritual books, perhaps a picture which has spiritual overtones. These will immediately signal to the helpee that it is all right to speak of spiritual things. In fact, they may produce the very opening for which a helpee was looking to discuss some particular aspect of the spiritual life.**

Space

The space between the helper and helpee as they sit down to talk is important. It should not be too distant nor too close, and differs from person to person. Each of us has about us a certain physical space which we claim—a leftover from the phenomenon of territoriality in animals. It is important to respect this space in the helpee. If she begins to push her chair back or pull it forward, the helper will know that the space is being readjusted for greater comfort. Experimentation in placing the interview chairs will eventually lead to a position which is fairly comfortable for most people.

Posture and Movement

The posture assumed by the helper should be relaxed but attentive. Also, it should be changed from time to time. To take up what one thinks is a good helper pose at the beginning of the interview and never change it for 60 minutes can be deadly. One is engaged in a living interview and will normally change posture in response to something the helpee has said. For instance, one will generally lean forward to convey greater interest or intensity. Such things as stretching one's legs out or crossing them in a manner which creates a barrier between helper and helpee should be avoided.

Eye Contact and Facial Expression

One should maintain regular eye contact with the helpee without staring. It is through the eyes that much of the non-verbal agenda is conveyed. Using swivel chairs for the interview, as previously suggested, provides a way of turning slightly, thus breaking eye contact in a natural way from time to time. One should also be aware that for certain cultures, maintaining eye contact with another can be disrespectful. The helper should always try to find out what lack of eye contact on the part of the helpee means.

With regard to facial expressions, one should try to be natural, matching one's feelings to one's facial expression where appropriate. Beginning counsellors often think that they must never show their feelings but maintain a completely objective stance, no matter what is said. This is usually not helpful and can even be read by the helpee as a lack of interest or care.

Time

Being physically present to the helpee means that one is not constantly preoccupied with time. Under ordinary circumstances, the helper should schedule interviews in advance and for a certain length of time which is known to the helpee. If the interview is an unscheduled one, the helper should indicate to the helpee at the beginning of the interview how much time she has. A clock should be placed in the interview room in such a position that the helper can see it without changing position. This eliminates the distracting gesture of looking at one's watch.

Gestures and Mannerisms

Extreme gestures and mannerisms can distract the helpee from what is being said. Gestures, when properly used, can highlight or emphasize a comment, but when exaggerated or repetitive are distracting. On the other hand, mannerisms such as pulling one's ear or scratching one's head are usually distracting and should be controlled as much as possible.

Voice

Quite aside from *what* is said, *how* a thing is said—the voice's volume, rate and overtones—are extremely important. A voice which is too loud can be threatening, whereas one which is too soft can be annoying and lead to misinterpretations. The proper voice is one which is clear and audible. Likewise, the rate of speech should be neither too hurried nor too slow since people who come for help often have trouble concentrating, and either way of speaking might result in losing them in very short order. Research done by Mehrabian and Ferris in 1967[1] showed some amazing results regarding the effect of verbal, vocal, and facial components in communication. According to their research, 55% of the message is conveyed by non-verbal facial expressions, 38% by verbal overtones and only 7% by the actual words which we say. As an example of how verbal overtones can change the whole meaning of a sentence, consider the difference in meaning of the following sentence if one emphasizes the highlighted word:

I didn't say **you** took the book.
I didn't say you took the **book**.
I didn't say you took the book.

We as helpers need to be aware of all of these voice components and be attuned to their effect upon the helpee.

Energy Level

Our energy level will directly affect that of the helpee. Helpers must learn to pace themselves in such a way that they are not so physically or psychologically tired when seeing people that they cannot give them their full attention. On the other hand, an extremely high energy level conveyed by such things as rapid speech, high-pitched tones, constant movement, etc., is also not helpful in that helpees often lack energy, and this tires them even more. Energy level should be such that one can stay respectfully alert through the whole conversation. This requires that the helper be aware of his or her own energy cycle. It may require such practical things as not scheduling interviews immediately after lunch or late in the evening.

2. Psychological Attending

The second skill in the Pre-Helping Stage is that of Psychological Attending. In addition to being physically present to the helpee, the helper must be psychologically present as well. There are many psychic factors which might alter the quality of the helper's presence to the helpee. Gazda lists some of these—one's needs, preferences, expectations, defense mechanisms, prejudices and fears.[2] Let us consider a few of the more important of these at greater length.

One's Needs

As humans we have needs. These have been researched at great length by people like Abraham Maslow. They include such things as the need to belong, the need for self-esteem, the need for achievement, etc. To expand upon the nature of human needs is not within the scope of this project. However, it is important to be aware that in both pastoral counselling and spiritual direction, the status of one's psychological needs impinges greatly on the quality of help being given. For example, if the helper has a high achievement need, she may try to manipulate the helpee in an effort to achieve what she sees as an appropriate goal for him or her. Or if the helper has an exaggerated need for acceptance, she may not challenge the helpee appropriately for fear that she may be rejected.

On the spiritual level, the helper may have a need to "convert" the helpee to her form of spirituality in order to affirm in herself that it is valid. This could block the natural progression of the helpee along a spiritual path which may be quite different from that of the helper.

There is nothing wrong with having needs. They are what inform us about the imbalances in our being. The important thing in helping relationships is to be aware of our own needs so that they will not interfere with the needs of those we are trying to help. To this end, the helper must take the time and employ whatever means are necessary in order to stay in touch with his or her needs and how these might be affecting the counselling or spiritual direction relationship. Taking time to identify and nurture their own needs is something which helping people are notoriously poor at doing. Yet it is essential if we are to help others to do the same.

One's Preferences

We all have psychological preferences which govern our ways of thinking and of acting. The widespread use of the Myers-Briggs Type Indicator (a personality indicator based on Carl Jung's personality theory) has brought this fact much to the fore in recent years. These preferences will most certainly affect the helping relationship. For example, a person who has a strong bent for logical thinking might well tend to jump too quickly to a problem-solving mode without properly exploring feelings. Extraverts might not give introverts enough time to process thoughts and feelings during the time of the interview, etc. Being aware of our preferences, especially those which are built right into our personality type, helps us to use them to enhance rather than block what is happening in the interview.

One's Defense Mechanisms

Just as we have automatic defense reactions which guard us against physical harm (e.g., blinking when something is thrown at us), so the psyche has "defense mechanisms" by which it protects itself against circumstances which may be perceived as threatening or hostile. Some of these mechanisms may become exaggerated and incorporated into a person's personality in such a way as to take on the nature of a conditioned response. Then, if the psyche is exposed once again to a similar combination of circumstances (inner or outer), one will tend to respond automatically in this conditioned way. Let us look at some of the most common defense mechanisms and their implications for pastoral counselling and spiritual direction.

i) Identification. Identification is something which is very important in our lives. In early childhood, for example, we identify strongly with the same-sex parent. As we grow, we begin to identify with certain groups, institutions and people. It is a mechanism which helps us define who we are and what values we will espouse. The difficulty lies in over-identifying with a particular person, group or object so strongly that we lose our own identity. For instance, an adolescent boy might so identify with his father that he fails to find his own identity as an adult but continues to live out the father's unfulfilled dreams.

> There are many ways in which over-identification may come into play in pastoral counselling and spiritual direction. One might, for example, so identify with the institutional Church that one could not be open to helping a person who has difficulty with some of its teachings. In such cases, the helper might end up defending rather than listening.

> On the other hand, identification with Christ is surely the goal of any Christian. It is this (sometimes unspoken, healthy identification) which must be present in the helper, and towards which one is guiding the helpee.

ii) Rationalization. In rationalization we "think up" or produce what we perceive to be acceptable reasons for an action, feeling or attitude which is not socially acceptable. For instance, someone might say, "I know that I drink too much, but if I didn't, I wouldn't be able to stand the pressures of my job," or "I didn't get the position because one of the people on the hiring committee has it in for me."

Rationalizations, if not confronted, will prevent growth since they are built on half truths or absolute falsehoods. They excuse rather than deal with inappropriate behaviors and attitudes.

> Important to both pastoral counselling and spiritual direction is the ability to uncover the truth that lies beneath both our own rationalizations and those of the helpee. Rationalizations are by their very nature so logical that they are sometimes hard to perceive. The disciple's famous statement at the anointing of Jesus at Bethany, "Why this waste? This could have been sold at a high price and the money given to the poor," seems reasonable on the surface, but what other motives might have been behind the statement? Could it have been a more acceptable

> way of saying, "We are embarrassed by this woman," or perhaps a way of rationalizing their own inattention to Jesus?
>
> Rationalization frequently rears its head in spiritual growth. We rationalize around behaviors or attitudes that we are afraid to relinquish. Yet we cannot grow spiritually if we do not let go of those things which are blocking us from growth in the Christian life. This letting go often plunges us into uncertainty, into a space where faith, not reason, must take pre-eminence. We must constantly remind ourselves of this fact as we journey with others in pastoral counselling and spiritual direction.

iii) Compensation. Compensation is a mechanism by which we substitute an achievable goal for a non-achievable or less-achievable one. The goal achievement often takes on an obsessive quality. For example, a young person who is not popular socially may compensate by being an over-achiever academically. Or a man who cannot stand up to his boss at work may compensate by bullying his wife.

Compensation can be a healthy defense, if properly used. People who are handicapped, for example, often compensate for their handicap by developing other skills. But if compensation is used to avoid facing the realities of one's life situation, growth will not occur.

> People may compensate for deficiencies in their lives by obsessive involvement in things "religious." Fanatic involvement in "causes," obsessive proselytizing, multiplied devotional practices to the exclusion of good works are some signs which must be monitored by both the helper and the helpee. These things block the free-flowing action of the Spirit and lead to the fulfillment of our own agendas, rather than God's agenda.

iv) Projection. Other people act as mirrors in whose behavior we see ourselves reflected. This is the basis for the defense mechanism known as "projection." Unfortunately, we do not always recognize our own reflection but attribute to others motives and attitudes which really lie within ourselves. For instance, a person who is obsessed with power will often ascribe that motive to the action of others, making statements such as, "The real reason that N. succeeds is that she is power-hungry." A manipulative person might see manipulation in the action of others. The test of whether a projection is occurring is that projections are usually accompanied by very strong emotions which are usually not commensurate with the situation which produced them. Projections can be either positive or negative and are useful in that they tell us much about what is going on within us at an unconscious level. But the helper must learn to identify projections within herself and within the helpee.

> In pastoral counselling and spiritual direction, the helper is usually someone who has espoused spiritual values and, in most cases, is a "good" person (whatever that might mean!). Helpees who have not recognized the goodness within themselves might tend to project their hidden desire for goodness on to the helper and make him or her almost a god. This can produce over-dependence and a distorted notion of "obedience" on the part of the helpee, causing him to hold every word that falls from the mouth of the helper as gospel.

v) Reaction Formation. In common parlance, this defense mechanism would probably be called "over-reacting." Whenever we sense that a reaction is not consonant with its cause, we are probably dealing with reaction formation. Over-reaction usually proceeds from fear of, or anxiety around, a certain event, attitude or behavior causing the person to react in a way which is directly opposite to the cause of the anxiety. For example, people who are anxious about change can over-react by becoming very rigid and unmoveable. A woman who suddenly discovers that she has been dominated by others during her whole life might over-react to any form of authority, even when it is legitimate. A pastoral counsellor or spiritual director might over-react to helpee behaviors which are not in keeping with his or her own value system.

Both the helper and the helpee must seek to discover the root causes of their over-reactions in order to keep the lines of communication open. Many people are intimidated by over-reaction, and unless one can recognize what is happening, the conversation may come to a halt, or one may find oneself reacting to the reaction.

> As a result of the changes in the Catholic Church initiated by Vatican II, the problem of reaction formation is often encountered by pastoral counsellors and spiritual directors. Moreover, in all Christian churches, new paradigms for the spiritual journey and the role of women in the Church, as well as in society, are emerging. We are also dealing in spiritual direction, and to a lesser degree in pastoral counselling, with spiri-

tual values which are deeply-held and upon which helper and helpee may sometimes disagree. All of this is fertile ground for reaction formation and must be recognized if dialogue is to continue.

3. Spiritual Attending

In pastoral counselling and spiritual direction, one must attend not only on a physical and psychological level but also on a spiritual level. This means that along with one's physical and psychological resources for listening, one listens also with the Spirit of God which resides in each one of us. To do this, the helper must try to be in touch with how the Spirit is moving within him or herself at any given time. One must attend in such a way that the God-life in me opens to the God-life in the other. This presupposes a life of prayer, a life which strives to be attuned to the Spirit in all things. One cannot isolate the helping interview from the rest of one's life in this respect. We must be attuned to the Spirit in an ongoing way. There is no such thing as turning the Spirit on and off during the time of the interview only. This ongoing attentiveness to the movement of the Spirit during the time of the interview is probably the most important "skill" of the whole model, as far as spiritual direction and to a lesser extent pastoral counselling are concerned. Without it, we take the "pastoral" out of the counselling and the "spiritual" out of the directing. It is the Spirit who must lead us in those things which go beyond the psyche. It is the Spirit who gives life which is ultimately what the helpee is seeking.

Notes

1. Mehrabian, A, and S. R. Ferris, "Inference of Attitude from Non-verbal Communication in Two Channels," *Journal of Consulting Psychology*, Vol. 6, 1967, pp. 109-114.

2. Gazda, op. cit., p. 24.

Exercises in Attending Skills

1. Physical Attending

Highlighting the Importance of Non-Verbal Cues

Before teaching non-verbal attending, have each trainee pair with another. In the dyad, they should place their chairs back-to-back and sit down so that they are not facing each other. Give them a topic to discuss for about 3 to 5 minutes. Then have them turn their chairs toward each other and continue the conversation for another 3 to 5 minutes. At the end of this time, bring all of the trainees back together and spend time processing the experience, being sure to note the differences they felt between the back-to-back and face-to-face experiences.

(This exercise is best carried out in a large room or with trainees in separate rooms so that there is no voice interference between the different pairs.)

Identifying the Various Elements of Proper Physical Attending

Choose one of the trainees to role-play with you (the teacher or trainer) an initial pastoral counselling interview. In the role-play, the pastoral counsellor should do all of the wrong things with regard to physical attending, i.e., chairs should be too close or too far apart, mannerisms should be exaggerated, voice tone should be too loud or too soft, telephone calls should distract, etc. The whole role-play should be exaggerated to bring out the different points.

After the role-play, trainees, through discussion of what was *not* helpful in the interview, are able to identify the various elements of proper physical attending.

Identifying Individual Attending Skills

Divide the group into triads. In each triad, have one person talk about a current interest or hobby, a second act as a listener and the third act as an observer. After about three minutes, the observer should give feedback to the listener as to his or her attending skills. Then the roles should be rotated so that each participant has had a chance to receive feedback on attending skills.

(Assuming that this is an initial training course, it is important at this point not to have trainees role-play an actual interview. Experience shows that this is too threatening for them at this stage, and they do not attend as they naturally would.)

2. Psychological Attending

Identifying Various Defense Mechanisms

a)   Having discussed the various forms of defense mechanisms during the sessions, ask trainees to choose one or two television programs during the week (soaps are good for this!) and see if they can identify any of the defense mechanisms discussed.

b)   If counselling tapes are available, choose one that illustrates some defense mechanisms and have students identify them, stopping the tape each time they do to discuss that particular behavior.

3. Spiritual Attending

Identifying the Leading of the Spirit

Ask trainees to take some time at the end of each day to reflect on how God has been present to them during that day. This can be done in the following manner:

a) Choose a regular time each day. (About 10-15 minutes are needed.)

b) Sit quietly in a private space.

c) Become aware of the presence of God in and around you and ask for the guidance of the Spirit.

d) Allow the major events of the past 24 hours to gently tumble through your mind, one at a time.

e) As each event or happening passes before your mind's eye, respond to God in whatever way seems appropriate. For example, you may want to thank God for a certain happening that day or conversely to vent your anger against God for something; you might like to ask for guidance around a certain event or be moved to a prayer of sorrow.

f)   Having gone through the individual events of the day, sit quietly for a few moments and be aware of your overall feelings about the day. Can you discern any particular theme, desire, urging through which the Spirit may be leading you?

g)   If you feel so-inclined, do some journalling about your reflections.

h)   End with a brief prayer of thanksgiving.

(This exercise, done on a regular basis, will enable the trainees to become better accustomed to attending to God in all things and thus better able to do so in the counselling or spiritual direction interview.)

Chapter Three

Stage I—Self-Exploration

As outlined in the overview of our model, the purpose of Stage I is to facilitate self-exploration on the part of the helpee. Often when people come for assistance, the presenting problem may not be the main issue at all. Therefore, the helper must give sufficient time to the process of exploration in order that the major issues become clear for both the helper and the helpee. Otherwise, one might move too quickly into an action which is not appropriate. In order to help the person in this task of exploration, the "Carkhuff-Gazda" model identifies three necessary skills:

1. Respect
2. Empathy
3. Warmth/Caring

Although both Carkhuff and Gazda place empathy first in listing the skills of Stage I, I prefer, for purposes of this work, to begin with the skill referred to as respect. I do this because I believe that in integrating the spiritual into this model, one must begin from a basic stance of respect for the other as created in God's image.

1. Respect

Respect in the context of this counselling model means that the helper believes in the ability of the other as a human being to resolve his or her own problems or issues. The helper acts only as a facilitator. Very often, beginning counsellors or spiritual directors fall into the trap of believing that they must be able to solve all problems and have the answer for every situation which they meet in their helping profession. This is not only false but it is detrimental to the helpee, placing him or her in a dependent role. Those who come to us for help very often have a poor self-image in the first place. Taking a problem out of their hands and solving it for them only serves to reinforce their poor self-image and make them more dependent. (It is recognized that there are certain crises situations in which the helper must initially take charge of the situation, but these are exceptions and will be treated later under the subject of referrals.)

George Gazda and his associates, building on the work of Robert Carkhuff, have developed what they call the "Respect Scale," a four-level guide for helpers, or those who are training them, to use in determining how proficient one is in this skill (Gazda, p. 196).[1] The types of responses typical of each level may be summarized as follows: (Level 1 shows the least amount of respect and Level 4 the greatest.)

Level 1: A response which *openly conveys* disrespect by
  a) dominating the conversation,
  b) imposing one's own values or beliefs on the helpee,
  c) immediately challenging the accuracy of the helpee's perception,
  d) devaluing the person by implying that he is incapable of handling the situation.

Level 2: A response in which the helper holds back by
  a) Ignoring,
  b) Responding in a casual way,
  c) Declining to enter into the helping relationship, thus implying that the helpee is not worth it.

Level 3: A response in which the helper demonstrates an openness to become involved in the relationship by
  a) Conveying the impression that the helpee is a person who has the ability to act constructively,
  b) Suspending judgment on what is said.

Level 4:   A response which conveys a willingness on the part of the helper to become involved and committed to the relationship by
a) Taking risks, and
b) Making sacrifices on behalf of the helpee, thus showing him that he is a person of worth.

The following examples will give some idea of how one can monitor the level of one's respect in responding using the principles outlined above.

Helpee Statement

"My kids are driving me crazy! They don't want to go to Church anymore; they don't want any curfews; they won't do anything around the house. I don't know what to do."

Possible Responses

Level 1:   "Surely you're making it sound worse than it is." (Instantly challenges accuracy of helpee's statement.) Or "That's certainly too big a problem for you to handle. Can't your husband take over?" (Devalues helpee by taking problem out of her hands.)

Level 2:   "That's too bad. Maybe you should get more involved in Church activities." (Ignores problem, declines entering into helping relationship, makes helpee feel unimportant.) Or "Don't worry, things will eventually get better." (Casual response devalues helpee's judgment.)

Level 3:   "It must be extremely frustrating for you. Why don't we talk a little more about it and see what your alternatives might be?" (Openness to become involved and respect for the person's ability to solve the problem.)

Level 4:   "Sounds really bad! I would be happy to work with you to try to find some solutions—then we can see where that leads." (Openness to become involved and willingness to make some sacrifices on behalf of the helpee, if necessary.)

When human beings were created, they were created in God's image and likeness—and God saw that they were good. (Genesis 1:31)[2] Surely we must acknowledge this basic dignity and goodness in our fellow human beings and express it in our respect for them. Each person has been gifted by God in marvelous ways. Often it falls to the lot of the pastoral counsellor or spiritual director to help persons uncover, recognize and accept their giftedness. This can easily escape them at times of vulnerability and woundedness.

One can grow in showing respect by paying attention to the points outlined by Carkhuff and Gazda, but the deeper respect that we owe each other because of the very nature of our being—a respect which must be the basic stance toward all those who come to us for assistance—must be cultivated in other ways as well. John of the Cross, in his writings on the spiritual journey, speaks of respect or esteem for neighbor as one of the marks of a person who has passed through the "dark night" and subsequently approaches life and prayer from a more contemplative stance.[3] The counsellor or spiritual director who is faithful to his or her own spiritual journey, living fully the darkness as well as the light, will somehow come to a deeper understanding of the dignity and worth of each human person and will carry this attitude into the helping relationship. This respect will then be communicated to the helpee, not only in the responses made, but in a deeper way which implies, "I believe in you as a person, wounded perhaps, but also gifted by God in ways beyond our imagining. Let us work together to uncover those gifts."

2. Empathy

Empathy is probably the most important of all the helping skills.[4] It means that one is able to put oneself in the shoes of the other, to understand at a very deep level the feelings and circumstances of the other. Empathy is not to be confused with sympathy, in which a person often takes on the emotion of the other. In empathy, the helper can feel for the other but still remain objective.

However, it is not enough to simply feel for another. One must somehow convey to him or her that both the *feeling* and the *content* of what is being said is understood. Carkhuff and his associates devised a method by which empathy can be taught and helpers' responses objectively rated. This is one of the most helpful tools for beginners in the helping professions. It dispels the myth that empathy comes naturally for some and is lacking in others. While it is true that some personality types find the skill of empathy easier to develop than others, all can learn from this model. Carkhuff, in his work, set up five levels of empathic responding. Gazda and his associates, drawing from Carkhuff, use four levels of empathic response with a numerical score or rating attached to each level. A summary of the four levels as laid out by Gazda is found in Table II.[5] Although empathy can sometimes be conveyed by a single word or phrase in response to a helpee statement, ordinarily it takes more than this to be of greatest value. The basic idea of an empathic response is to take what the helpee has said, identify the surface and underlying feelings contained therein, and present it back to the person in different words so that he can hear what he has said from a different perspective. It is also a way of checking whether or not one is really in tune with what the helpee is saying.

Let us expand somewhat on the use of the above scale by taking a helpee statement and giving some possible responses to it.

Helpee Statement

"I used to pray regularly, but since God took my son from me, I don't care if I ever pray again."

Possible Responses

Level 1: "That's terrible! You simply have to keep praying."
This is a Level 1 response because it completely ignores the feelings of the helpee. It is judgmental and therefore hurtful. The helper imposes his agenda on the helpee.

Level 2: "Prayer is no longer a value for you." This is a Level 2 response because it picks up only partially the feelings and content of what the other has said.

Level 3: "The death of your son has caused you to lose all interest in prayer." This is an accurate reflection of content and surface feelings, but does not get at the underlying feelings.

Level 4: "You blame God for the death of your son and that makes you so angry that you can't pray."
This response gets at the underlying feelings of the helpee. It conveys to the person that the helper understands at a very deep level how the helpee is feeling.

Table II: Empathy Scale

	Rating Scale	Key Concepts
4.0	A response which goes beyond surface feelings to identify and reflect underlying feelings.	Underlying feelings reflected.
3.5		
3.0	A response which accurately reflects surface feelings.	Surface feelings reflected.
2.5		
2.0	A response which only partially reflects surface feelings.	Partial reflection of feelings.
1.5		
1.0	A response which does not reflect even surface feelings. It could be hurtful or irrelevant.	Fails to reflect feelings.

(Adapted from Gazda, p. 88)

Note: Although it is not necessary to reflect the content of every helpee statement, its inclusion in the helper's response can either lower the level of responding if it is inaccurate or raise it if it is accurate. For example, a response that only partially reflects feelings but accurately reflects content may be rated at 2.5 rather than at 2.0.

One can readily see from the above example how much more effective a Level 3 or 4 response would be than a Level 1 or 2 response. Although even professional counsellors will sometimes respond with a Level 1 or 2 response, one should aim at an average Level 3 manner of responding when using the skill of empathy.

One of the blocks to the development of the skill of empathy is our paucity of vocabulary when it comes to describing feelings. Both Carkhuff and Gazda have developed lists of "feeling" words which are helpful in developing the skill of empathy. If one has difficulty in this area, it is highly recommended that these be consulted.[6] As previously mentioned, the skill of empathy is so important that beginning pastoral counsellors and spiritual directors should take time to systematically practice its use. I have found no better way of helping people to do this than by using the suggested Empathy Scale (Table II, p. 23) in the ways suggested in the exercises at the end of this chapter. Trainees may find these methods awkward during the initial stages of training but in time, responding with empathy will become natural for them and its effectiveness will be well worth the effort put into its development.

Empathy is closely related to that virtue which was the hallmark of Jesus' life and which I have used in the title of this work, that is, the virtue of compassion. One of the differences is that theoretically, empathy could be used simply as a skill without engaging the heart and prompting one to action in the same way as does compassion. Compassion implies a greater identification with the joys and sufferings of the other than does empathy, but this does not mean that, in its practice, one loses objectivity. What does happen is that compassion informs and deepens the quality of the empathic response. One of the ways in which Webster's dictionary defines compassion is, "spiritual consciousness of the personal tragedy of another or others and selfless tenderness directed toward it."[7] It is this spiritual consciousness of another's sufferings, as well as of their joys, which enables the helper to get into not only the mind and feelings of others but into their very heart.

And so, just as in the psychological realm empathy is considered by many to be the most important of the counselling skills, so in the spiritual realm, compassion in its fullest sense, is that attitude of mind and spirit which is the sine qua non of Christian care-giving. It is that quality of God-likeness, that common ground, where we can truly meet and stand with the other.

3. Warmth/Caring

As noted above, the skill of warmth or caring flows naturally from the skill of empathy. As we come to understand a person at deeper levels, our caring grows. This, of course, needs to be communicated in some way to the helpee. Most expressions of warmth are communicated non-verbally—through the eyes, through caring touch, posture, etc. If the voice is used to express warmth, it is not so much what we say as the tone used in saying it which is important.

Although scales have been developed for rating warmth, I believe that it is something which is very hard to rate numerically in a trainee. Its mode of expression is so particular to each person and to each situation that one can only judge its presence or absence on the basis of the whole interview.

Warmth must be genuine. It cannot be forced and is very much dependent upon the response of the helpee. People who have not experienced much warmth in their lives may be frightened off by too much warmth too early in the relationship. Warmth expressed through touch requires particular skill in timing and judgment. It is rather a tragedy that in our touch-starved society, abuses regarding touch have caused us to become less spontaneous and probably less healing in this regard. Gazda (p. 111) gives some good pointers regarding the use of touch in a helping relationship. He says that the two most important factors to remember are the level of trust between the two persons and whether or not the touch is perceived by the other person as sexual. Touch, when properly used, is a very powerful tool in the helping relationship.

In an article in *Human Development* entitled "Empathy is at the Heart of Love,"[8] James Gill points out the reciprocal nature of empathy and love. In dealing empathically with a person, one comes to know that person at a very deep level and this usually results in loving that person. Conversely, if one loves a person, it is much easier to be empathic with that person.

The basis of the Christian message is love:

"You must love the Lord your God with all your heart, with all your soul, and with all your mind... You must love your neighbor as yourself." (Matt. 22:37-40)
and
"Love one another as I have loved you." (John 15: 12)

It follows that as pastoral counsellors and spiritual directors grow in living out this commandment of love, they will grow in their capacity for empathy and in their capacity for warmth and caring. Hence, the importance of growing in the Christian virtues at the same time as one is developing one's helping skills.

Thus we see how the skills of Stage I can be deepened by the Christian virtues and attitudes to which they are related. Respect, Empathy, Warmth—the skills used by the helper in establishing trust and enabling the helpee to honestly explore a situation—correspond amazingly with the Respect, Compassion and Caring which Jesus practiced in his ministry.

Notes

1. All rating scales subsequently referred to are from George M. Gazda, Frank S. Asbury, Fred J. Balzer, William C. Childers and Richard P. Walters, *Human Relations Development: A Manual for Educators*, Third Ed., Copyright 1984 by Allyn and Bacon and are used with permission.

2. All scripture quotations in this work are from *The Jerusalem Bible*, Reader's Ed. (New York: Doubleday & Co. Inc., 1968).

3. Kavanaugh, Kieran and Otilio Rodriguez, *The Collected Works of John of the Cross* (Washington: ICS Publications, 1973), p. 324.

4. See Carkhuff, R.R., "Selection and Training" in *Helping and Human Relations: A Primer for Lay and Professional Helpers*, Vol. 1 (New York: Holt, Rihehart & Winston, 1969), p. 202.

5. Gazda, op. cit., p. 88.

6. For lists of feeling words consult the following: Carkhuff, R.R., *The Art of Helping*, Fifth Ed. (Amherst, Mass: Human Resource Development Press, 1983), p. 255 ff. and Gazda, George, op. cit., p. 235 ff.

7. _____ *Webster's Third New International Dictionary* (Springfield: G. & C. Merriam Co., 1971), p. 462.

8. Gill, James J., "Empathy is at the Heart of Love," *Human Development*, (New York: Jesuit Educational Center for Human Development, Vol. 3, No. 3, Fall, 1982), pp. 29-41.

Exercises in Stage I Skills

1. Respect: Training in Rating Responses on the Respect Scale

Instructions

Divide the trainees into small groups of three or four people and have them together rate on the Respect Scale the possible responses to the helpee statements given in each of the examples below, remembering the key words that identify each level.

Level 1 - Dominates, imposes, devalues
Level 2 - Witholds
Level 3 - Open
Level 4 - Involved, committed (Gazda, p. 96)

Remember also that the essence of respect is believing in the person, i.e., believing that the helpee has the human potential to resolve his or her own issues.

After the small groups have rated the responses, bring them back together to see how their results compare and to discuss any differences of opinion.

Helpee Statement One

Woman to pastoral minister:

"My husband insists that I spend all my time at home with the children. I don't know what to do."

Possible Helper Responses

_____ 1. "Perhaps you should leave him."

_____ 2. "I know your husband. I'll talk to him."

_____ 3. "That's too bad."

_____ 4. "That's a tough situation! Want to talk about it?"

_____ 5. "A lot of husbands are like that."

_____ 6. "You probably feel quite helpless, but perhaps if we talk about it, we can arrive at some solution to the problem."

_____ 7. "You want to, and feel that you could be doing things outside the home as well."

_____ 8. "Guess you'll just have to put up with it."

_____ 9. "Why don't we talk a little more and see what we can come up with."

_____ 10. "I'm willing to spend some time discussing this if you think it would be helpful."

Helpee Statement Two

Pastor to associate pastor:

"I'm sick and tired of doing all the work around this parish. Everyone complains, but nobody wants to help."

Possible Helper Responses

_____ 1. "You think you're having a hard time! Let me tell you what's happening with me."

_____ 2. "It's not a pleasant situation."

_____ 3. "Want to talk about it?"

_____ 4. "You've handled some pretty difficult situations before. Care to brainstorm some of the techniques you used in those situations?"

_____ 5. "You might as well forget about it. You can't do anything about it anyway."

_____ 6. "They are lazy, aren't they!"

_____ 7. "It must be discouraging when you put so much effort into it and no one seems to respond."

_____ 8. "Why don't you talk to the bishop? Maybe he'll move you."

Instructions to Trainee

Following are some helpee statements. Read each carefully, then write a response which seems natural for you. Rate your response on the Respect Scale and, if it does not meet the criteria of a Level 3 response, rework it until it does.

Helpee Statements and Helper Responses

1. Parishioner to pastor:

   "When the parish council meets, I never get to talk."

   Response: _____

   _____

   _____

2. Parish worker to colleague:

"I don't know what I did to offend Mrs. Jones, but she won't talk to me."

Response: _____

_____

_____

3. Seminary intern to clergy supervisor:

"I'm not sure that I will be able to meet people at the back of the church. I'm so shy!"

Response: _____

_____

_____

4. Unemployed man to pastor:

"I've never been out of work before in my whole life. I'm just lost!"

Response: _____

_____

_____

5. Woman to pastor:

"I'm so angry that our parish won't allow girl altar servers! My daughter is hurt over it and I don't know what to tell her."

Response: _____

_____

_____

In the above exercise, trainees should formulate their responses individually, either in class or as a homework assignment. Various responses should then be discussed in the whole group.

2. Empathy: Rating Empathic Responses

Instructions to Trainee

Several helper responses are given to each helpee situation below. Rate each on the Empathy Scale as outlined on page 23. In each situation, imagine that the statement is being made to you as a pastoral counsellor.

Helpee Statement One:

"My wife and I had a fight last night. Somehow it was different from our usual fights. I thought for a minute I was going to hit her."

_____ 1. "That frightened you!"

_____ 2. "You know you'd never do that."

_____ 3. "At other times when you've fought, there was less animosity?"

_____ 4. "Maybe you should break up your marriage."

_____ 5. "You were very angry."

_____ 6. "Your anger just took over, and that frightens you."

_____ 7. "You're very confused."

_____ 8. "You're frightened because you don't understand why you reacted differently this time."

_____ 9. "You're shocked that you could even think about hitting your wife."

_____ 10. "That must be scary! It's as though you don't know what you might do if you get into another fight."

Helpee Statement Two:

"I'm sick and tired of cooking and cleaning up after everybody. I never have any time for myself and nobody even cares."

_____ 1. "You feel used!"

_____ 2. "You would like people to at least notice what you are doing."

_____ 3. "You're angry because you have to do all the work and never get to do the things you want to do."

_____ 4. "Maybe you should take a holiday."

_____ 5. "What a depressing situation."

_____ 6. "You've always done the things you thought you should be doing and now you find you're just being taken for granted.

_____ 7. "Why don't you get a maid?"

_____ 8. "That must be extremely frustrating—never-ending work, no time for yourself, and on top of it all, no recognition."

_____ 9. "I've felt that way myself at times. I know just what you mean."

_____ 10. "What would happen if you just stopped doing the work?"

Helpee Statement Three:

"I think I'm losing my faith. God is just like everyone else—never around when you need him."

_____ 1. "You don't believe God cares for you."

_____ 2. "No one, including God, is giving you support right now."

_____ 3. "You thought that at least God would be faithful, even if everyone else deserted you."

_____ 4. "You're tired of everyone deserting you when the going gets tough."

_____ 5. "Your faith is important to you."

_____ 6. "It's bad enough when those you counted on desert you, but when God deserts you, that's the last straw.!"

_____ 7. "You shouldn't feel that way about God."

_____ 8. "So all your friends have let you down."

_____ 9 "You're angry at God."

_____ 10. "You thought that you and God were on better terms."

Having rated the responses in the above exercises individually, bring the group together to discuss how their ratings compare with those of the others in the group.

Identifying Surface and Underlying Feelings

Empathy, as we have seen in the text, deals with both surface and underlying feelings. The following exercise is designed to give the trainee some practice in identifying feelings at both levels and giving an appropriate response.

Helpee Statement One:

Woman to pastor:

"I don't know what to do with my son anymore. If he keeps hanging around with that gang, he'll end up in jail. I thought I had raised him better than that!"

Surface Feelings _____

Underlying Feelings _____

Appropriate Response (at Level 4) _____

_____

_____

Helpee Statement Two:

Woman to pastoral minister:

> "Tom told me last night that he thinks we should end our marriage. I know we've been having difficulties, but I never dreamed he was thinking of that."

Surface Feelings _____

Underlying Feelings _____

Appropriate Response (at Level 4) _____

_____

_____

Helpee Statement Three:

Parishioner to president of parish council:

> "I'm fed up with this committee work. It seems I'm knocking my head against a brick wall trying to get anything done."

Surface Feelings _____

Underlying Feelings _____

Appropriate Response (at Level 4) _____

_____

_____

Helpee Statement Four:

Parishioner to priest:

> "It's not easy to grow old. No one takes you seriously anymore."

Surface Feelings _____

Underlying Feelings _____

Appropriate Response (at Level 4) _____

_____

_____

Helpee Statement Five:

Woman to spiritual director:

> "I used to like going to Church, but since we moved into this new parish, I dread going to Mass on Sunday. I don't know anybody there."

Surface Feelings _____

Underlying Feelings _____

Appropriate Response (at Level 4) _____

_____

_____

Practice in Responding With Empathy

Divide the group of trainees into triads. In each triad, have one act as helper, one as helpee and one as observer. Have the helper and helpee role-play a pastoral counselling situation in which the helper responds empathically to each statement of the helpee, insofar as this is possible. The helper should not ask a lot of questions nor get into a problem-solving mode. The observer should rate the helper's responses on the Empathy Scale and give feedback after about five minutes. The helpee should also give feedback as to how he experienced the helper with regard to empathy.

Practicing and Rating Empathic Responding

If audiotaping or videotaping equipment is available, have the trainees work in pairs to tape a pastoral counselling interview. This can be a role-play or an actual situation. (If role-playing is new for the trainees, they will usually find it easier to enact a real situation from their past or present life.) Each trainee should take a turn at being the helper.

After the taping has been completed, have each trainee transcribe the tape in which he or she acted as helper and rate each of the responses on the Empathy Scale, giving reasons for the particular rating given in each case.

3. Warmth, Empathy and Respect

Have trainees examine the manner in which Christ related with people, as recounted in the four gospels. If there are a number of trainees, the group could be subdivided and a different gospel assigned to each sub-group. Trainees should be asked to find one or two examples of how Christ exhibited each of the skills of Stage I (respect, empathy and warmth) in his relationships, noting any ways in which the use of these skills might differ in a *pastoral* setting. The trainees' findings should be discussed in the next class or meeting.

Chapter Four

Stage II—Self-Understanding

The purpose of the Stage II skills is to help the person grow in greater self-understanding. Having explored the problem or issues and accurately identified what needs to be addressed, one utilizes additional skills to help the person go deeper. Respect, empathy and warmth, the skills of Stage I, are now used along with helper skills outlined by Carkhuff and Gazda for Stage II—Concreteness, Genuineness and Self-disclosure. To these I have added a fourth—Prayer—so that in our model, the skills of Stage II are:

1. Concreteness
2. Genuineness
3. Self-disclosure
4. **Prayer**

1. Concreteness or Specificity

This skill is one which enables the helpee to be more exact and narrow things down so that she can come to a greater understanding of the problem or issue being discussed. Once again, Gazda sets up four levels of responding using the skill of concreteness (Gazda, p.147). These are summarized as follows:

Level 1:   A response which is vague or inaccurate.

Level 2:   A response which tends to intellectualize the problem rather than helping to focus it.

Level 3:   A response which models specificity by leading the person to be more specific.

Level 4:   A response which openly asks the person to be more specific.

To illustrate this, let us examine the following example.

Helpee Statement

"They say that we should be more involved in social justice and that makes me feel funny."

Possible Responses

Level 1:   "They certainly don't know what they are talking about, do they?" (Does nothing to clarify the response. It still remains vague.)

Level 2:   "Well, social justice is an issue in the Church today. We should be involved." (Intellectualizes the problem and takes it out of the realm of the helpee's experience.)

Level 3:   "There are some people who talk about social justice and when they do, you experience feelings that you can't label." (Models specificity leading to more specificity on the part of the helpee.)

Level 4:   "Who are they?"
"What does social justice mean to you? —to them?" "What does 'funny' feel like—guilty? —angry? —confused?" (These responses aid the helpee in being more specific about each part of the statement.)

Once again, timing is important in the use of this skill. If the helper demands too much specificity too early in the interview, it may come across as some sort of a cross-examination. One must allow the helpee room to explore in the initial stages of the relationship. This is why the skill of concreteness is placed in Stage II of the model. (Concreteness should not be confused with data-gathering, i.e., such things as social history, previous experience of spiritual direction, etc., which are usually done at the very beginning of the helping relationship.)

2. Genuineness

Genuineness means simply what the word implies—the helper is genuinely him or herself in responding to the helpee. One does not try to fit into some sort of stereotypic role of pastoral counsellor or spiritual director. The helper does not sit, for example, like an emotionless sphinx, always "maintaining objectivity" despite the sometimes horrendous nature of what the helpee is relating. One is allowed to show appropriate feelings, provided they do not interfere with the helping process. Genuineness on the part of the helper will encourage the helpee to be more genuine and lead to deeper understanding.

3. Self-disclosure

Self-disclosure is a very important skill, but one which must be used with discretion. Some people have a story to match or exceed whatever situation a person is presenting: "I know just what you mean, something like that happened to me once . . ., etc." or "That reminds me of the time when. . ., etc." These kinds of responses are rarely helpful. They come off as one-upmanship and make the helpee feel inferior, ignored, or distanced. On the other hand, self-disclosure, properly used, can be very powerful. The rule of thumb is that it should be helpful to the helpee and relevant. It is important to note that self-disclosure is a Stage II skill and is not generally used until a trusting relationship has been established through the skills of Stage I. In fact, self-disclosure may never be used in a particular helping relationship if there is nothing in the helper's experience which is relevant to the helpee's situation.

Another skill which is needed at this stage for pastoral counsellors and spiritual directors who are approaching the helping relationship from a faith perspective is that of Prayer. I shall first speak of the use of prayer in pastoral counselling, then go on to show how this differs somewhat in spiritual direction, at least in its initial use.

4. Prayer

As was indicated above, the purpose of Stage II is to help a person achieve a greater self-understanding. One of the most powerful means that we have to do this is through prayer. The importance of prayer in understanding the psychological as well as the spiritual self is addressed by Ann and Barry Ulanov in their book *Primary Speech: A Psychology of Prayer.* They maintain that prayer is our "primary speech," the most fundamental of all languages, a language which is common to all human beings, whether they know it or not. It is "the most direct line of communication we have to our interior reality."[1] And it is in prayer that "energy to improvise and imagine different courses of action and ways of seeing things comes to us."[2] Those of us who have been spiritual directors for any length of time know that this is true, that people do reach extraordinary depths of self-understanding through prayer. This is the reason for including prayer at this point in the model.

Although one hesitates to label prayer as a skill, the way in which the helper brings prayer into the whole helping process certainly requires great skill. Like many of the other skills, the use of this one will be very particular to each helper. When it comes to the gift or skill of prayer, one cannot bluff. In order to use prayer effectively in the interview, it must be part of the helper's life.

Often pastoral counsellors ask if they should begin the interview with prayer. One should not assume, because one is operating within a faith context, that this is always a good thing to do. A lot depends on the faith background of the helpee and the nature of the issues being discussed. Another reason for placing prayer in Stage II of our model is that one must, through the use of Stage I skills, first get a sense of the helpee and whether or not including prayer as a part of the interview per se would be helpful. If one makes the judgment that the helpee is in fact a person who is open to the explicit introduction of prayer into the sessions, there are several ways in which this can be done.

(1) The helper may suggest that the interview begin with prayer. This can take various forms—rote prayers which are familiar to the helpee; spontaneous prayer on the part of the helper and/or the helpee; a short scriptural reading or a few moments of silence, allowing both helper and helpee to center in God. Whatever form it takes, it should not be forced but

should be something with which both helper and helpee are comfortable.

(2) Another way of using prayer as a means of facilitating self-understanding is through prayerful ritual. Particularly helpful are rituals centered around the need to let go of things in one's life that are blocking deeper self-understanding. The helper must be alert to the proper timing of such rituals and reflect with the helpee on how the ritual has helped in the area of self-understanding.

As an example of what is meant, I was once counselling a young man who had a lot of psychological baggage which was blocking him from the deeper self-understanding necessary for him to move on in freedom in his life. I asked him to think about the things that were holding him back and to design some kind of prayer ritual which might help him to let go of these things. What he did was to gather a number of stones of various weights. On each he wrote one of the things which he perceived as holding him back, matching the weightiness of the issue to the relative weight of the stone. Then he chose some appropriate passages from scripture and together we sat on the shore of the lake as he took the stones, one by one, talked about each of the issues involved and threw each stone into the lake. As it turned out, there was one that he could not let go. It was an area of his life which we had touched upon and thought we had resolved but in fact, needed much more work. It was only in the ritual that that became clear to both of us.

(3) One may choose to pray at the end of the interview rather than at the beginning. This too is a place where spontaneous prayer can be very powerful. Often it becomes a reflection on the insights of the time together, leaving the helpee with the sense that he is not alone in the journey but has within himself the Source of understanding and wisdom which may be tapped into at anytime. It acts as a good transition between the interview and the ongoing life of the helpee.

(4) Finally, unlike the other skills, the skill of prayer is one which the helper must consciously use outside the time of the actual interview. If we believe in the efficacy of prayer, then we must believe that, if we take those whom we are assisting with us to prayer (figuratively, that is!), God will help us in our companioning. If at the end of each day, one simply holds up to God in prayer each person one has journeyed with that day,

it is amazing what helpful insights emerge. One should do this with unhurried gentleness, expecting nothing in particular but open to whatever comes. If one does gain certain insights in prayer regarding a particular helpee, these can be presented to the person at the next interview. The helpee will probably be pleasantly surprised to learn that your concern for him or her goes beyond the time of the actual interview. And once again, it will model for the helpee the necessity of using prayer as one of the resources for coming to a deeper understanding of self.

Although most of what has been said about prayer in the above paragraphs will apply to spiritual direction as well as to pastoral counselling, there is one big difference. Unlike pastoral counselling, in spiritual direction it is assumed that prayer is an integral part of the person's life and should be discussed in the spiritual direction relationship. What is the directee's concept of prayer? How does this fit in with the director's concept of prayer? Do different attitudes towards prayer present any blocks to a productive relationship? These are things which must be discussed and reflected upon in order to determine the suitability of a particular director for a particular directee.

The Global Scale of Responding

Before proceeding with the skills of Stage III, it is appropriate at this point to speak of another scale presented by Gazda and his associates in their helping model, that is, the *Global Scale* of responding (Gazda, p.115). This scale was developed as a means of rating the helper's overall manner of responding during an interview. Once again, Gazda presents four levels of responding as follows:

Level 1: A response which is *harmful*

Level 2: A response which is *ineffective* or irrelevant

Level 3: A response which is *facilitative* or helpful

Level 4: A response which is *additive* in some way

The use of this scale is a very effective way of objectively rating the quality of communication on the part of the pastoral counsellor or spiritual director. It takes into account all of the skills presented in this model. Individual helpers will develop these skills in their own unique ways, but no matter how different their styles are, all can be objectively rated using this scale.

In judging the effectiveness of one's responses, the Global Scale can be used in the following manner:

Record and transcribe an interview.

Consider each helper response in turn, asking oneself the following questions:

a) Was the response helpful?
   If so, rate the response at the 3 Level.

b) Was the response more than helpful? Did it *add* something to the interview, give a new insight, reveal underlying feelings, etc.? If so, rate the response at the 4 Level.

c) If the response was not helpful, was it hurtful?
   If so, rate the response at the 1 Level.

d) If the response was not helpful, but not hurtful, then rate it at the 2 Level.

Effective pastoral counsellors and spiritual directors should be operating at an *overall* 3 or 4 Level, although there will be occasional times when even experienced helpers will give a 1 or 2 Level response.

In the teaching of this model, the Global Scale of responding can be used as a rating instrument at any point after the skills of Stage I have been taught and practiced. I have found it best to use this scale after teaching the skills of Stage II. This gives wider scope for the discussion of why a certain response was helpful, harmful, etc. For instance, a response may be helpful because it uses the skill of *concreteness* effectively or gets at underlying feelings in a perceptive way (*empathy*). Or it may be irrelevant because it is an inappropriate *self-disclosure* or lacks *warmth*.

Use of this scale helps to integrate all of the skills presented in the model into one's personal style of helping.

Notes

1. Ulanov, Ann and Barry, *Primary Speech: A Psychology of Prayer* (Atlanta: John Knox Press, 1982), p. 6.

2. *Ibid.*, p. 100.

Exercises in Stage II Skills

1. Practice in Combining Stage I and Stage II Skills

Instructions

Arrange trainees in a double circle, as illustrated in the diagram, with one trainee positioned in the center as the helpee. The helpee begins a role-play with one of the helpers in the outer circle. They continue with the role-play for several minutes, at the end of which time the helpee turns to the next helper who continues on with the role-play. The same procedure is followed until the helpee has talked with each of the helpers or until the issue being role-played is resolved.

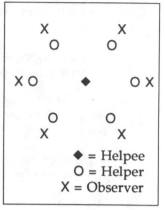

♦ = Helpee
O = Helper
X = Observer

Each observer keeps track of the dialogue between the helpee and the helper assigned to him or her and rates each response on the Global Scale.

At the end of the role-play, the observers in turn give their feedback and the whole group enters into discussion of the ratings and any other helpful observations.

Audio/Videotaping

If audiotaping or videotaping equipment is available, have the trainees work in pairs to tape a pastoral counselling interview. This can be a role-play or an actual situation. Each trainee should take a turn at being the helper.

After the taping has been completed, each "helper" should transcribe his or her tape and rate each of the responses on the Global Scale, giving reasons for the ratings and naming the particular skill used in each response.

2. Self-Counselling Exercise

Have trainees choose an area of concern which they have with regard to their personal life or their counselling abilities and, in written form, counsel themselves around that area. In their responses to "self" they should use only the skills of Stage I and Stage II, avoiding the action or problem-solving skills which come in Stage III.

Example:

Self: I'm not sure that I will be an effective pastoral counsellor. I can't seem to get into my own feelings, let alone interpret the feelings of others.

Response: You tend to be more cognitive in your response to life.

Self: Exactly! Give me a problem to solve and I'm happy, but I'm not that good at handling people.

Response: And that scares you!

Self: Darn right it does! I'm afraid I'll just bulldoze over peoples' feelings and miss the point of what they are experiencing.

Response: You're doing a pretty good job of expressing your feelings right now.

Self: I am, aren't I! But this is different.

Response: Different? In what way?

etc., etc.

When the dialogue has been completed, trainees should rate each of their responses on the Global Scale, giving reasons for the rating and telling what skill is being used.

3. Identifying the Use of Prayer in the Helping Relationship

Have trainees write short reflection papers in response to the following questions:

a) How does prayer enter into Jesus' ongoing helping relationships?

b) How does prayer enter into your ongoing helping relationships? (This can include other than *formal* helping relationships—i.e., those that occur in the course of everyday life.

Chapter Five

Stage III—Action

The purpose of Stage III is to facilitate some kind of action or resolution on the part of the helpee. The skills that are added at this point are Confrontation and Immediacy. In some adaptations of the model, Support is added as a third skill (Egan, 1975). To Support, I have added the element of supportive Christian Community. And so the skills of Stage III are:

1. Confrontation
2. Immediacy
3. Support (Involving Christian Community)

1. Confrontation

For many, even the *word* "confrontation" has negative connotations. People often consider confrontation as some sort of personal attack against which they must put up defenses. As a result, this is generally what happens and people very often do not hear what is being said.

One should take special note of where confrontation fits in this model. It does not appear until Stage III. One must have established a solid relationship with the helpee, and he or she must have moved into a deeper level of self-understanding before confrontation will be effective. In fact, some studies actually show that negative feedback (a form of confrontation) is *never* helpful (Jacobs, 1975).[1]

In this model, confrontation can be defined as "the pointing out of or calling attention to discrepancies." This may be discrepancy between:

a) Two things which the person is saying which are contradictory.
   e.g., 1st Statement—"I love the Mass."
   2nd Statement—"I never go to Mass."

b) What the person says and what he or she does (or fails to do).
   e.g. Statement—"Punctuality is a value for me."
   Action—She is 15 minutes late for each session.

c) The way the person experiences herself and how others experience her.
   e.g., Self-experience—"I'm a totally incompetent person."
   Experience of Others—She is very competent.

Following are some guidelines which may make confrontation or feedback concerning discrepancies more palatable. The desired outcome is that the person will *act* in some way to change the behaviour or the attitude if it is detrimental to growth.

Guidelines for Feedback[2]

a) Feedback should be descriptive rather than judgmental or evaluative. For example, "Are you aware that you have interrupted Mary three times since we started?" is better than saying, "You're a very rude person, the way you interrupt people!"

b) In giving feedback, one must be specific, not general. To tell someone she is an angry person without giving a specific example of how this is manifested is not helpful.

c) The needs of both giver and receiver must be considered in giving feedback. One does not confront another just to make oneself feel better. The helper must judge at any given time whether or not the person can handle the feedback and whether or not it will be helpful.

d) One does not give feedback about something which is beyond a person's means to change at the time. For instance, to tell a depressed person that their belief in God's loving providence is inconsistent with their depression may only cause feelings of guilt.

e) Since feedback is accepted better when it is requested, an agreement about the giving and receiving of feedback should be a part of the ongoing relationship. This can best be done by talking about it at the beginning of the relationship.

f) Feedback is most helpful when well-timed. The closer the feedback is to the experience, the greater it is in intensity. If one wishes to make the confrontation less intense, one should wait for what seems an appropriate time to give it.

g) It is wise to check with the helpee to see if she has really understood what has been said.

h) It is well also to remember that positive feedback should be given whenever possible. In fact, if one finds it necessary to confront a person, it is wise to begin with an affirmation of the other's strong points. Studies show that in most cases affirmation will more readily promote growth than will negative feedback. (Jacobs, 1975)

Responses to Feedback

The helper needs to be aware that people will react differently to feedback. Gerard Egan, in his book *The Skilled Helper*,[3] discusses the following possible reactions:

a) Discrediting the confronter by pointing out some of the confronter's negative behaviors.

b) Rationalizing his or her behavior.

c) Making light of what is being said.

d) Seeking support from others in order to show the confronter that he is wrong.

e) Agreeing with the confronter, but doing nothing about it.

f) Taking the feedback seriously and examining its ramifications, with the aid of the helper.

If the helpee reacts in any except the last way listed above, one can assume that there is something wrong in the wording, timing or intensity of the confrontation. Referring back to our helping model, we can probably assume that the goal of Stage II (self-understanding) has probably not yet been realized. The helper must then ask himself the question, "Do I need to go back and spend more time with this person in self-exploration (Stage I), in order to facilitate greater self-understanding?" (Stage II)

How is confrontation informed by the spiritual? If one is trying to live out of the deeper levels of one's being, trying to keep in touch with the sacred in all things, one is more apt to recognize discrepancies in the other, particularly as they affect that person's life in God. In pastoral counselling and spiritual direction, one is dealing not only with discrepancies at the psychosocial level but with discrepancies which touch the level of lived faith. If the helper is not a person of deep faith himself, many of these discrepancies will escape him.

Confrontation has to do with truth. As one grows in one's knowledge of the God who is Truth, one also grows in one's sensitivity to truth in general. But, in the context of a helping relationship, truth which is confrontative must be well-timed and well-worded. It must also be based in love. We often hear the injunction, "Speak the truth in love." This love goes much deeper than the "caring" spoken of as one of the Stage I skills. It is, as explained earlier, the very basis of our relating in Christ. Confrontation or loving feedback in the light of our common bond as Christians becomes a responsibility for the health of the whole living Body of Christ.

2. Immediacy

Immediacy is that skill by which the helper monitors what is really going on between the helper and the helpee at any given time during the course of an interview or during the course of the relationship in general. Immediacy addresses the often unspoken elements of the relationship, such as suppressed anger, projection, the development of dependency, etc. Many of these things, if not dealt with, will block the growth of the helpee and the ability of the helper to properly guide him. If, for example, the helper senses that the helpee is holding back anger at something which has been said, he might interject with, "I seem to be picking up some anger. Does it have to do with what I just said? Perhaps you would like to talk about it?"

Dealing with the unfolding dynamics of the ongoing relationship itself is sometimes harder than dealing with an individual remark or isolated feeling within an interview. Such things as "falling in love" with the helpee or vice versa, extreme personality clashes, or deep divisions regarding value systems call for a considered and skillful use of the skill of immediacy. It is for this reason that this skill is placed in Stage III. Premature use of this skill in an ongoing relationship can be destructive of helpee and helper alike. On the other hand, immediacy properly timed and sensitively worded can keep the relationship both facilitative and honest.

> **Just as in the skill of confrontation, in-touchness with one's total being, including one's spiritual being, makes one aware of discrepancies in the other, so does it make one more sensitive to the unspoken reactions of the other. If one is living the "sacrament of the present moment," one will be very attuned to what is happening at all levels of the present and thus will pick up more readily on the use of the skill of immediacy.**

3. Support

Having journeyed with the helpee to the point of action facilitation, it is important that the helper be there to support her in whatever action is taken. Sometimes moral support is all that is necessary. At other times, one must become an advocate for helpees, teaching them how to make their way through the bureaucratic maze which often surrounds access to other helping agencies. Referral too can be unfamiliar territory for many. It is important that people be helped through the sometimes arduous steps of this process, being careful, however, not to take it out of their hands. In the initial stages of this new relationship, support through occasional contact is also important. (The whole matter of referral will be dealt with at greater length in a subsequent chapter of this work.)

Although we are dealing here with support as one of the skills of the *helper*, he or she can extend that support by identifying with the helpee the components of the particular support system within which the helpee is operating—i.e., family members, co-workers, friends, various support groups, etc. These are different for each person. Some will have come to light during the course of the pastoral counselling or spiritual direction relationship. It is good, however, to more intentionally draw them all together at this point in order to reassure the helpee that he or she is not alone in carrying out the decided-upon action.

How does one support another spiritually? The various ways which we have already discussed of bringing the spiritual into this model are in themselves supportive of the ongoing spiritual growth of the helpee. In addition one has all of the resources of the Christian community to draw upon for help. The Christian community is called to support the weak, the ill, the discouraged, the frightened and suffering members of its community. We, as helpers, should make the helpee aware of the various forms of support which have been set up within the parish or diocesan community—such things as groups for the grieving, for the separated and divorced, for troubled teenagers, etc.

In spiritual direction, one can give support by making available to the helpee information regarding ongoing faith-development programs, books, faith groups, retreat opportunities, etc.

Outside of the support offered in prayer, probably the most important way in which a pastoral counsellor or spiritual director can be supportive of those with whom they journey is by being faithful to their own faith journey. Lawrence Kohlberg, in discussing movement from one stage of moral development to the next,[2] stresses the importance of modelling in that process.[4] How one models faith is a rather intangible thing but that one models faith is something which we have all experienced in our own journeys. At times of doubt and vulnerability, how reassuring and supportive it is to find someone who is "faith-full," whose commitment to God and to the ups and downs of the journey gives us the hope that we need to continue faithfully in ours. I once had a spiritual director who had been afflicted with polio in youth and later by multiple sclerosis. Through all of this, he continued to live out his life with a faith and cheerfulness which spoke to me much louder than the words which passed between us. No matter how big my problems might be at the time, I always emerged from our talks with the certain knowledge that there was a power beyond ourselves which could and would support us through the worst (and best!) of times.

We have referred to this last Stage of the model as the Action Stage. If the helper has used the skills of all three stages well, it is to be hoped that the helpee will arrive at an appropriate action on his or her own. "Action" here can refer to minor behavioral changes or attitudinal changes, as well as action in respect to major life changes. This is often the case in spiritual direction where, for instance, one may emerge from a directed retreat knowing that, in one sense, nothing has changed but in another, everything has changed. The action has taken place internally.

As mentioned at the beginning of this work, pastoral counsellors and spiritual directors often panic because they think they have to solve the problem for the helpee. This is not so. The task is to facilitate the helpee in arriving at an appropriate action. However, there are a few simple techniques which can be used by beginning pastoral counsellors and spiritual directors at various stages of the helping relationship to aid the helpee in arriving at an appropriate action. I have included some of these in Appendix A of this work.

This brings us to the end of the discussion of our model per se. Those who are engaged in pastoral counselling on a full-time basis will need to move on from this model to learn more extensive intervention techniques in the particular area in which they will be specializing. However, because this work is directed mainly toward those for whom pastoral counselling is not their full-time work (those I have referred to as "occasional pastoral counsellors") and toward spiritual directors, another topic must be addressed—referral counselling. This I shall do in the following chapter.

Notes

1. Jacobs, A., "Research on Methods of Social Intervention: The Study of the Exchange of Personal Information in Brief Personal Growth Groups," Paper presented at the Invited Conference on Small Group Research, Indiana University, Bloomington, April, 1975.

2. Domzall, Raphael, Paraphrase of notes presented at a workshop on "Health, Growth, and Human Relations," Xavier University, Cincinnati, 1980.

3. Egan, Gerard, op. cit., p. 168 ff.

4. Kohlberg, Lawrence, *The Philosophy of Moral Development: Moral Stages and the Idea of Justice* (San Francisco: Harper & Row, 1981).

Exercises in Stage III Skills

1. Confrontation

Following are several situations in which confrontation is called for. Divide the trainee group into triads of helper, helpee and observer and have them role-play one or more of these situations, the helper carrying through with the actual confrontation. After each scenario, observers should give feedback and suggestions as to the effectiveness of the confrontation and the helpees should tell how they felt in the face of the confrontation.

Situation One

You are a pastoral minister working with a pastor who has a drinking problem. You are generally on good terms and he seems to respect you. Lately, however, his drinking has been getting worse and some of the parishioners have approached you because they have noticed that the pastor "acts strangely" at some parish meetings and sometimes even at Eucharist. They say that he laughs inappropriately, talks incessantly, and just does not seem to be himself. You know (and probably they know!) that this is his pattern when he has been drinking. You feel that you have to confront him.

Situation Two

One of the members of the parish council is constantly monopolizing the weekly meetings. The chairperson has tried in vain to remedy the situation and has asked you, the pastor, to confront this person whom you know fairly well.

Situation Three

The secretary in the parish to which you have recently been assigned as associate pastor has held her present job for about 20 years. She knows everyone in the parish and has decided to take you, "the rookie," under her wing. She is constantly screening your calls, telling you that she knows the complainers and that there is no use in your wasting your time with them. She is always checking to see where you are going and giving you unsolicited advise regarding not only parish affairs but even about your personal life. You are fed up!

2. Immediacy

Role-Playing Immediacy

Using the same format as above, that is helper, helpee, observer triads, role-play the following situation using the skill of immediacy to resolve the difficulty.

Situation

A young woman has come to you several times for counselling regarding her marriage. Although the particular problem which brought her to you in the beginning has now been resolved, she continues to call you, asking for time just to talk. You see her another couple of times, but feel that the interviews are going nowhere and that she is using them simply as an excuse to see you. You know that you must deal with this situation.

Identifying Present Feelings

The purpose of this exercise is to help trainees to monitor and name their present feelings, making them aware of how these can change from moment to moment. Hopefully, this will enhance their use of the skill of immediacy during an interview situation.

Have trainees sit in a circle of not more than eight people. (If there is more than one group of eight, they should be in separate rooms or be widely enough separated so that there is not voice interference from one group to another.) Participants should close their eyes, relax and try to identify their *present* feelings. One person begins by saying aloud, "Now I feel . . .," naming the present feeling or emotion. After a minute or so, the next person in the circle uses the same formula, noting his or her present feelings. This procedure continues, going around the circle several times. Afterwards, all participants should take time to process the experience together.

3. Support

Identifying One's Current Support System

As a homework exercise, have each trainee reflect upon his or her current support system. Both individuals and groups should be identified, along with the type of support each offers. In the subsequent class, in groups of three or four, have trainees share some of their findings and discuss the impact of this exercise upon each of them.

(Having carried out this exercise, trainees will be better able to assist helpees in identifying their support systems.)

Chapter Six

Referral Counselling

For pastoral counsellors, such as priests and pastoral workers, for whom this ministry is only one among many, it is imperative that they be proficient in the art of referral counselling. They have neither the time nor, in most cases, the expertise, to engage the helpee in ongoing therapy. Yet both research and practice have proven that for most churchgoers, the first person to be approached in times of difficulty or crisis is the parish priest or minister. Spiritual directors, too, must be skilled in referral counselling since many of the people who seek spiritual direction are initially in need of psychological counselling as well.

I shall first present some general principles regarding referral counselling and then point out ways in which its relationship to pastoral counselling differs from its relationship to spiritual direction.

1. Whom Should One Refer?

In general terms, one should refer anyone who can be helped more effectively by someone else. Helpers who naively think that they are capable of effectively helping all who come to them will do more harm than good. In fact, for those who work in parishes, the vast majority of people who come to them for counselling help will need to be referred.

In determining who should be referred, we might separate them into three broad categories determined by:

The Time and Training of the Helper

- those who do not benefit from short-term counselling (five or six visits)

- those in need of deeper psychological help—the depressed, the suicidal, the psychotic, etc.[1]

The Nature of the Problem

- those who need the help of specialized agencies such as A.A., family agencies, associations for the handicapped, etc.

- those who need group support such as bereavement groups, groups for the separated and divorced, etc.

- those who need medical assistance

- those who need financial counselling

Interpersonal Dynamics Between Helper and Helpee

- those who are blocked because of an unresolvable personality clash between the helper and the helpee

- cases in which the helper has a strong sexual attraction for the helpee, which stands in the way of objectivity

Some good questions to ask oneself when in doubt as to whether or not to refer might be:

"Can I help this person, in this situation, with the skills I possess and in the time I have available?"

and

"Should I be referring this person to a specialized group or agency that has more experience and expertise in this matter than I have?"

2. Where and How to Refer

Essential to the art of referral counselling is a knowledge of the helping people and agencies available in the immediate area. Identifying the network of helping people available is one of the first things the helper should do when moving into a new situation. Following are some practical suggestions for doing this:

1. In any new placement or assignment, always check to see what helping resources have traditionally been used there and if they are still adequate.
2. Check to see what resources are available through the local schools—e.g., counselling resources, vocational guidance, etc.
3. Visit the local hospital and inquire about pastoral and social services, psychiatric resources and crisis teams.
4. Most large cities have directories of all the helping agencies and mental health resources available in that city. These can be traced down through the local library.
5. It is well also to have the name of at least one medical doctor (preferably a general practitioner) to whom people can be referred if they have no family doctor.
6. If possible, one should have on hand the names of some competent counsellors, psychologists and psychiatrists to whom people can be referred. These should be practitioners who will respect the religious values of the persons referred.

In referral counselling, it is not enough to have lists and names of resource people and agencies. One should, if possible, have personal knowledge of how they function. It is therefore adviseable to make personal contacts with as many of these resources as possible. Helpees are much more open to referral if the helper has personal knowledge of the agency or person to whom they are being referred. Howard Clinebell has some excellent suggestions regarding *how to refer* persons. Following is a condensed and paraphrased version of his suggestions:

1. Create the expectation of referral early by making clear to helpees the parameters of your role as a *pastoral* counsellor, and offering to assist them to find the right service if that becomes necessary.
2. Start where the persons are in their perceptions of the issues being discussed and try to bring their perceptions as close to

those of the counsellor's as possible. This will more easily permit referral.

3. When referring persons, interpret for them the general nature of the help they may expect to receive and help them to resolve any emotional resistance they may have.

4. Establish strong enough rapport with helpees to develop a bridge over which they may walk into another helping relationship, and let them know that one's pastoral care and concern will continue after the referral.

5. Encourage referred persons to give a therapist or agency an honest try, even if they are only mildly interested.[2]

In the art of referral (which indeed it is!), one must be careful not to refer too soon nor to wait too long. Beginning pastoral counsellors, not trusting their skills, sometimes tend to panic and refer a person before they have adequately explored the nature of the problem. On the other hand, some pastoral counsellors tend to hold on too long, moving into issues beyond their capacity to solve and making referral more difficult as the person becomes more dependent on the relationship itself. A delicate balance between panic and prudence is what is required.

> Often priests and ministers who do only part-time pastoral counselling, in their anxiety over possible deficits in their counselling skills, tend to forget that they have much to offer in the healing process. They are professionals among other professionals in the helping field. Their expertise lies in the spiritual realm which is often the very realm that people need to deal with in order to be healed. This does not mean that they try to cover up psychological problems with pious platitudes. What it does mean is that in the counselling relationship, they bring to bear the vast spiritual and theological riches of the Church—the wisdom gleaned by holy people throughout the ages and the healing power of the sacraments. Many who come for pastoral counselling and/or spiritual direction have lost a sense of meaning in their lives. If they are "religious people," they cannot ignore their roots. They need to re-connect and often re-interpret what that means for them. This is where the pastoral counsellor or spiritual director has expertise. This is where they must confidently step forward and offer their skills to a wounded world.

Referral counselling is somewhat different for spiritual directors than for pastoral counsellors—not in its basic principles but in its timing. People do not generally come to spiritual directors for psychological counselling. It is, therefore, sometimes more difficult for the spiritual director to bring a particular directee to the realization that psychological problems may be blocking progress in the spiritual life and that these need to be attended to either before or during the course of spiritual direction. Again, this dilemma can be circumvented if the spiritual director clearly defines the limits of his or her role early on in the relationship, thus creating the possibility of referral if the course of the relationship so dictates.

Generally speaking, spiritual directors have not received as much training in psychology as have pastoral counsellors. They should, therefore, readily refer those in serious psychological need to therapy or other specialized agencies. Whether or not spiritual direction continues during this time depends on the nature of the referral and the desire of the directee. In those cases where it is deemed advantageous to continue spiritual direction at this time, the spiritual director must be aware of the nature of the help being given by the other person or agency in order that they not be working at cross purposes. To this end, it may be helpful for the pastoral counsellor or spiritual director to communicate directly with the person or agency to whom a person is referred. This is always done with the knowledge and consent of the helpee.

Another thing that spiritual directors must consider is the type of spirituality to which the directee seems called and where the person is in the spiritual journey. Just as pastoral counsellors are unable to help everyone who comes to them, so spiritual directors cannot relate to the spirituality of everyone who seeks them out. An extraverted charismatic, for example, might have difficulty directing an introverted hermit, or someone who is very new at spiritual direction might have difficulty directing those who are seasoned in the journey. What is important in spiritual direction is that both director and directee feel very free both initially and as the relationship progresses to look at the suitability of the match. Probably the easiest way to do this is to contract with the directee during the initial interview for a set period of ongoing direction (probably about six sessions), at the end of which time, director and directee will evaluate together the efficacy of the relationship. The director should make clear to the directee that she will not be hurt if they decide that another director would be more suitable.

In spiritual direction, it is not always up to the director to make a referral to another spiritual director. Sometimes the directee has another person in mind or she may not feel the need to continue in direction at that particular time. So unique is each person's spiritual journey that one must be very free in this regard, allowing the Spirit to lead the person wherever God is calling.

Conclusion

This brings us to the end of our consideration of the proposed model. Learning to use this model is like learning to play a piece on the piano. Each skill is like a phrase of music which must be practiced over and over again before it fits smoothly into the whole. Phrases which some musicians may find easy, others will find more difficult. But with perseverance each musician is finally able to produce a work of art in which the individual movements and phrases blend one into the other without effort and the musician is able to add his or her own interpretation to the piece as a whole.

So too, when one has practiced individually the various stages and skills of this model, one can put them together in a way that is unique to oneself. Different helpers will stress different parts of the model and use the skills in different ways as they become more comfortable in "playing the tune."

It is important that those who are trainers help trainees to identify their own particular counselling style—their way of using these skills to bring harmony where there was discord, hope where there was despair and the healing peace of Jesus Christ to troubled hearts. Lest we hesitate in this task, we have the reassuring words of St. Paul to support us:

"Glory be to God whose power working in us can do infinitely more than we can ask or imagine."

Eph. 3:20

Appendix A

Some Useful Techniques for Helping

In this section I will present in a very cursory fashion some simple techniques for helping people at various stages of the model discussed in this work. Numerous books have been written which treat of each of these methods in detail. These can be pursued at greater length by helpers who will be practicing more extensive therapy in their ministry. But for purposes of this work, I believe it is enough to alert the "occasional counsellor" and/or spiritual director to the existence of these techniques and point them to some sources which will allow them to do further research and study in the areas of their choice.

1. Obtaining a Data Base

In order to raise consciousness to the frequency and circumstances of certain behaviors in the helpee's life, the helpee might be asked to keep a daily journal noting:

   a) how many times this behavior or attitude occurred,
   b) under what circumstance, and
   c) the feelings surrounding that behavior.

This will help to identify patterns of behavior which can then be dealt with in the pastoral counselling or spiritual direction relationship.

This exercise, if done in the context of prayer, is similar to what used to be called the "Examination of Conscience" and is more currently referred to as the "Consciousness Examen," the difference being that this exercise focuses on only one area of the person's life at a time. I have found that this is a good thing to do in spiritual direction as well as in counselling, particularly if the directee is dealing with a specific problem which seems to be blocking spiritual growth. By beginning the exercise with a prayer to the Spirit for enlightenment, trying to stay aware of God's presence during the exercise and ending with a prayer of thanksgiving, one can convert a psychological technique into a prayer experience.

2. Writing Therapy

(Used here to include any writing which is aimed at enhancing growth and healing)

Writing therapy can be used in numerous ways in the course of the pastoral counselling or spiritual direction relationship. Some people who find difficulty expressing their thoughts or feelings verbally are more able to do so in writing. Even persons who can express themselves well can sometimes touch into deeper levels of their consciousness through writing. Following are some circumstances in which writing therapy could be used:

To express anger:

Helpers can sometimes "let off steam" in an emotional situation by sitting down and writing exactly how they are feeling without censoring their writing in any way. Allowing a free-flowing, stream-of-consciousness type of reaction to emerge on paper often releases tension and gives a person the necessary time to cool down and think more rationally about possible reactions to a situation. This type of writing, shared with the helper over the course of a pastoral counselling or spiritual direction relationship, can give much insight into the emotional state of the helpee.

To bring closure to certain relationships:

Sometimes people suffer and are unable to move forward in life because they have not been able to communicate their thoughts and feelings to a loved one who is now dead. In such a case, the helper might ask the helpee to write a letter to the loved one and say all those things that have not been said. Reading the letter out loud to the helper and allowing time for any emotional reactions which may emerge to be dealt with can be very therapeutic in such a situation.

As an aid to enhancing communication in a broken relationship:

Some persons find it difficult to express their feelings verbally to another with whom they have had or are having difficulties. In such cases, the helpee might compose a letter to the other person, putting on paper all those things which he or she might wish to say to the other. This letter-writing alone might give the helpee enough courage and clarity to deal verbally with the situation. If this does not happen, the helpee could actually give the letter to the person concerned and ask to discuss it with him or her at an appropriate time.

3. Imaginative Dialoguing

Myriad books are now being written on the various ways in which one can engage the imagination in healing dialogue. The use of the imagination as a healing tool is not new. It is used in such things as dream work, gestalt therapy, exercises in healing of memories and is basically the starting point for the type of prayer known as Ignatian Contemplation. More recently, it has been used extensively in "inner child" work.

At appropriate times in the course of the helping relationship, the helpee might be asked to set up in his or her imagination a dialogue between:

i) different parts of the self which seem to be in conflict;

ii) herself and an emotion which needs to be explored; (This is done by asking the helpee to either personify the emotion or think of a symbol for it with which she can dialogue.)

iii) the helpee and another person with whom there are strong, unresolved issues.

This dialoguing can be done in various ways. Following are a few suggestions:

a) It can be done in the pastoral counselling or spiritual direction interview itself. The helper may invite the helpee to relax, close her eyes, imagine the person or symbol with which she will dialogue and begin the dialogue in her mind. She may either speak the words of the dialogue aloud or carry it on in silence. In either case, the helper and the helpee, upon completion of the dialogue, process the experience together.

b) The helpee may be invited to do some imaginative dialoguing around a certain issue before the next session. In this case, the person may either write down the dialogue as it is happening or simply engage the imagination in dialogue and write down the effects of the dialogue to be shared with the helper at the next session.

> In both pastoral counselling and spiritual direction, it is sometimes wise to ask the helpee to invite Jesus into an inner dialogue which might otherwise become particularly frightening for him or her.

Dialoguing as a technique is most helpful at Stage II of the above model, where the helpee is trying to come to a deeper self-understanding. It can also be used in decision-making (Stage III) where a person is struggling with a choice between two possible responses to a situation. I will speak of this further under the topic of decision-making below.

4. Identifying Patterns and Themes

During a helping session and throughout the course of a helping relationship, helpers will do well to listen carefully for *recurring* themes, patterns and concerns voiced by the helpee. These might take the form of such things as self-denigrating statements, constant blaming of others, immediate negative reactions to certain subjects, etc. The accent here is on the *recurring* nature of such reactions and behaviors, which is often a clue to something that needs to be dealt with at a deeper level. When such a pattern is discovered, the skill of immediacy can be used to bring it to the attention of the helpee.

5. Decision-Making / Discernment

Decision-making or discernment, in the sense of trying to make wise decisions about how God is acting in one's life, comes at the end of the model presented above. If the helper has used the skills outlined in a proficient way, the action or decision to be taken will often emerge from the process itself. At other times, some additional help is needed to come to a final decision. Following are a few which I have found helpful:

Tracing Patterns of Decision-Making

Ask the helpee to go back over the major decisions of his or her life and reflect upon what it was like before, during and after each decision. The following questions are a guide for the helpee to reflect upon and should be responded to in writing so that they can be brought to the helping session for discussion.

a) What were the circumstances leading up to the decision?
What were your feelings prior to making it?
What aids did you use in helping you come to the decision?
How long did it take you to make it?

b) How did you feel when you finally made the decision?
What steps did you take to implement it?
What, if any, were the *immediate* changes that took place in your life as a result of the decision?

c) After the decision was implemented, how did you feel?
What were the long-term results for you of making that decision?

Having done this exercise, the helpee can then discuss the results with the helper. Together they endeavor to identify those patterns of decision-making which have been beneficial or harmful to this particular person in the past and how this learning can be applied to the present decision.

Engaging the Body in Decision-Making

When a decision involves a choice between two distinct possibilities, one can use the following method:

Ask the helpee to close his eyes, breathe deeply and relax. Then ask him to imagine *in detail* all of the ramifications for himself of choosing one of the alternatives. In his imagination, have him put himself into the actual situation that would occur as a result of that choice and note his *bodily* response to the situation. After allowing adequate time to explore all aspects of that particular choice and their impact on the body, helper and helpee can discuss the experience. The same procedure is then followed for the alternative choice, noting again the bodily response and comparing the two experiences.

In the past, we have too often relied on logic alone in our decision-making. We have not taken into account the valuable information which our bodies can give us. It is, after all, our bodies which must live out the consequences of our decisions, and they are wise indicators of what the decision may cost in terms of emotional and physical well-being. Having used the above approach many times in my practice, I can attest to the dramatic results it can produce when logic and some other types of prayerful discernment have not produced the desired answer.

Once a decision has been reached using this method, the helpee might spend some time in prayerful presence before God, testing whether or not the decision carries with it the peace of the Spirit.

Another way of engaging the body in decision-making is to have the person dialogue aloud with herself around the particular issue. To facilitate this process, two chairs are set up facing each other. The person concerned begins by sitting in one of the chairs and, facing the other empty chair, states some of the reasons why she would make the decision in a certain direction. She then moves to the other chair and responds to herself, taking the opposite view. The dialogue continues with the person moving from chair to chair as she debates the merits of each of the possible choices.

Usually, in this type of exchange, one position emerges more strongly than the other. As the dialogue is in progress, the helper notes the emotional overtones which accompany each position. These observations are brought into the discussion as the exercise is processed with the helpee at the end of the dialogue.

Ignatian Discernment

Ignatian discernment is sometimes wrongly interpreted solely as a way of helping one choose between two definable alternatives. For the uninitiated, it can become just another problem-solving technique—a way of isolating the pros and cons of a given course of action. While Ignatius does present us with a method of decision-making which considers the spiritual advantages and disadvantages of a possible choice, the notion of discernment is much broader. It entails an ongoing commitment to the task of discerning God's presence or discovering how God is directing a person in all of the circumstances of his or her life. Within this context, the Ignatian method of decision-making referred to above can be very effective.

Rather than try to replicate descriptions of this method, which have been drawn up by those who are much better versed in Ignatian spirituality than am I, I have included at the end of this chapter some references which will be helpful for those who wish to use this approach. I particularly recommend the little book *Orientations*, Vol. 1, by John Veltri, S.J., which deals with this and other approaches to discernment.

Each Christian care-giver will in time and through continuing education discover action techniques appropriate to him or herself. Some of the above techniques may uncover psychological baggage which cannot and should not be dealt with by care-givers who have not been trained in psychology. In these cases, the appropriate course of action is a referral as set forth in Chapter Six of this work.

Some Helpful References

Capacchione, Lucia. *Recovery of Your Inner Child.* New York: Simon & Schuster, 1991.

English, John J. *Choosing Life.* New York: Paulist Press, 1978.

Evoy, John J. *A Psychological Handbook for Spiritual Directors.* Kansas City: Sheed & Ward, 1988.

Fanning, Patrick. *Visualization for Change.* Oakland: New Harbinger Publications, 1988.

Green, Thomas H. *Weeds Among the Wheat, Discernment: Where Prayer & Action Meet.* Notre Dame: Ave Maria Press, 1984.

Halpin, Marlene. *Imagine That! Using Phantasy in Spiritual Direction.* Dubuque, Iowa: Wm. C. Brown Company Publishers, 1982.

Veltri, John A. *Orientations, Vol. 1: A Collection of Helps for Prayer.* Guelph: Loyola House, 1979.

Appendix B

Answers to Rating Exercises

Respect Scale

Helpee Statement One			*Helpee Statement Two*	
1.	1.0		1.	1.0
2.	1.0		2.	2.5
3.	2.5		3.	3.0
4.	3.0		4.	4.0
5.	2.0		5.	1.0
6.	4.0		6.	2.0
7.	3.0		7.	3.0
8.	1.5		8.	1.5
9.	4.0			
10.	3.0			

Empathy Scale

Helpee Statement One

1.	3.0
2.	1.0
3.	3.0
4.	1.0
5.	2.5
6.	3.5
7.	2.5
8.	4.0
9.	4.0
10.	3.5

Helpee Statement Two

1.	4.0
2.	3.0
3.	3.0
4.	1.5
5.	3.0
6.	3.5
7.	1.5
8.	3.0
9.	1.0
10.	1.0

Helpee Situation Three

1.	3.5
2.	3.0
3.	3.5
4.	2.5
5.	2.0
6.	4.0
7.	1.0
8.	1.5
9.	2.5
10.	3.0

Bibliography

Carkhuff, Robert R. *The Art of Helping,* Fifth Ed. Amherst: Human Resource Development Press, 1983.

Carkhuff, Robert R. "Helping and Human Relations: A brief guide for training lay helpers." *Journal of Research and Development in Education.* Vol. 4, No. 2 (1971a). pp. 17-27.

Carkhuff, Robert R. and W. A. Anthony. *The Skills of Helping.* Amherst: Human Resources Development Press, 1984.

Carkhuff, Robert R. *The Art of Helping: Student Workbook.* Amherst: Human Resources Development Press, 1985.

Egan, Gerard. *The Skilled Helper: A Model for Systematic Helping and Interpersonal Relating.* Monterey: Brooks/Cole Publishing Co. Inc., 1975.

Egan, Gerard. *The Skilled Helper: Model, Skills, and Methods for Effective Helping.* Monterey: Brooks/Cole Publishing Co., 1982.

Egan, Gerard. *Exercises in Helping Skills.* Monterey: Brooks/Cole Publishing Co. Inc., 1975.

Gazda, George M. et al. *Human Relations Development: A Manual for Educators,* Third Edition. Toronto: Allyn and Bacon, Inc., 1984.

Gill, James J. "Empathy is at the Heart of Love." *Human Development,* Vol. 3, No. 3 (Fall 1982). pp. 29-41.

Clinebell, Howard. *Basic Types of Pastoral Care & Counselling: Resources for the Ministry of Healing Growth.* Nashville: Abingdon Press, 1984.

Jacobson-Wolf, Joan E. *When to Counsel, When to Refer: A Diagnostic Manual for Clergy on Mental Health Referral.* Lima, Ohio: C.S.S. Publishing Co., 1989.

Jones, Alexander, Ed. *The Jerusalem Bible: Reader's Edition.* New York: Doubleday & Company, 1968.

Kavanaugh, Kieran and O. Rodriguez. *The Collected Works of St. John of the Cross.* Washington: ICS Publications, 1973.

Kohlberg, Lawrence. *The Philosophy of Moral Development: Moral Stages and the Idea of Justice.* New York: Harper and Row, 1981.

Maslow, Abraham H. *Toward a Psychology of Being,* Second Edition. New York: Van Nostrand Reinhold Co., 1968.

Ramsperger, Frank. *Free to Grow.* Guelph: Loyola House, 1976.

Ulanov, Ann and Barry. *Primary Speech: A Psychology of Prayer.* Atlanta: John Knox Press, 1982.

Notes